THE JESTER H

The Jester Hennets

EDMOND LEO WRIGHT

HARRY CHAMBERS/PETERLOO POETS

First published in 1981
by Harry Chambers/Peterloo Poets
Treovis Farm Cottage, Upton Cross, Liskeard, Cornwall PL14 5BQ

ISBN 0 905291 25 5

Printed in Great Britain by
Latimer Trend & Company Ltd, Plymouth

Acknowledgements

Grateful acknowledgement is made to the Bodleian Library, Oxford for permission to reproduce the cover illustration of King David With Fool from MS. Douce 18, f.113ᵛ. (*Psalter. Book of Hours. Use of Sarum.*)

Harry Chambers/Peterloo Poets
receives financial assistance from
The Arts Council of Great Britain

REVISED NOTE ON THE HENNET:

The hennet consists of a 12-line verse rhyming abacbcdedeff, each line of 11 syllables. Their scansion is a development of the classical hendecasyllabic.

CONTENTS

*   *   *   *   *

'Now Your Sentence, My Liege!' ...

'Now your sentence, my liege!' the minister said.
'Rascals like this deserve the worst!'—At this, Rex,
(Jester Extraordinary), popped his head
up from behind the Bench right beside the King's.
'Minister! Do you think execution checks
crimes such as theft and rape? Can't you manage things
rather better? This rascal's father now, why
shouldn't we punish him? *He's* the one to blame!'—
'Yes, of course,' said the King, 'the *father* must die!'
'Wait though,' said Rex: 'what about the Mayor? The same
goes for him!'—'Yes, of course,' said the King, '*him* too!'—
'Then, King, off with your head—the same goes for you.'

9

'Genuflection's The Thing!' ...

'Genuflection's the thing!' said the King. 'When you
pass by my picture, all must kneel—at least bend,
nod your head—everyone must give me my due.
Prime Minister first, the Chancellor, then all
go in turn. Where my image is, I extend
self as if real. What stands for me, you must call
me, wherever it is, sovereignty striking
awe in the least of its forms!' So they went,
one by one, past the picture, genuflecting
humbly before it, until Rex came, who bent
down in front of a footman: 'Lord, here's thy due!'—
'What's this?'—'Lord, your reflection's here in his shoe.'

.

The Prime Minister said 'My Lord—' 'Yes?' said Rex, ...

The Prime Minister said, 'My lord—' 'Yes?' said Rex.—
'Fool, hold your tongue!' said the King. 'He is able
to tell who is the King!'—'But without his specs,
King, he might mix us up. It's easy for me!'—
'You can see my crown, Fool!'—'But there's no label
on it, for can't you see mine?'—'Well you can see
the throne, can't you?'—'Wouldn't want me to bow
down to a mere lump of gold!'—'But look, it's been
made for me!'—'No, for me. Look, King, you'll see how
any old backside will do.'—'Enough! My queen
can see! Here's my sceptre and my orb! Have done!'—
'Here's my sceptre and two orbs—you've only one!'

'Above All Laws Must Be Clear! ...

'Above all laws must be clear! my royal purpose,
plain in its universal wisdom, be spelled
out in detail so no one rebellious,
lazy or sly can pretend that ignorance
can provide an excuse! so all are compelled,
yea, forced to be free!'—'A word, Your Impudence,'
Rex in the humblest of tones broke in. 'For me
there's a snag. Since I'm longing for you to guide
such a fool as I am, can I please now see
all those instructions of yours by which I'm tied?
I've one problem much too ticklish to handle:
at what angle should I stick up my candle?'

'I Am Sickened By Clinging Minions ...

'I am sickened by clinging minions whose
claim to be here in my court rests entirely
on a title! He puts on his father's shoes,
walks in and bows and scrapes for his kitchen scraps!
I can't even decide who is to hand me
coffee at breakfast. See them wag their foolscaps
as they bob up and down to protocol's tune!
Give me a man, not a name! Give me a deed,
not a word!—Hey! What's this, you buffoon?'—
Rex had crept up: already one shoe was freed,
had been thrown in the air. 'What a pong, eh?—Whew!
but still, give me a kingly foot, not a shoe!'

At The Feast The Prime Minister Said...

At the feast the Prime Minister said, 'My lord
King, O it gives me great pleasure here to declare
just how much all your subjects are in accord.
Love of their monarch! That is the talisman
that makes one of us all! What would we not bear,
would we not suffer? Every citizen
would accept any pain, any anguish to
prove how we love you!'—Up jumped Rex with 'Alack,
sire, his love's less than mine! Where is your thumbscrew?
Here is my thumb! For my aching back your rack
is the remedy! Any mill I can tread?
Oh I love you so much!—Please chop off my head!'

The Physician Had Asked The King To Inspect ...

The Physician had asked the King to inspect
how he was carrying out his onerous
duty to safeguard the nation, to protect
all from infection, how he wielded his lancet.
Not a poisonous air, not a cancerous
fiend but would yield to his knowledge of planet
or his talent with knife. The King deigned to go,
saw his mixing of herbs, his diagnosing
from the stars. At the end, the King cried, 'Bravo!'
as he sawed through a patient's leg. 'Amazing
genius! Well done!'—Rex too cried, 'Bravo! Well done!
Just for the King, please saw off the other one!'

At The Grand Soirée...

At the Grand Soirée all praised the King's playing.
'Never has flute warbled so divinely sweet!'—
'Oh, your majesty, I was only saying
here to the maestro how you put him to shame!'—
'All those confident trills! No one can compete,
sire, with true genius!'—'Why, my lord, your fame
exceeds every professional!'—'Oh encore!
Let us hear more!'—At which Rex cut a caper
round the music-stand, snatched away the King's score,
singing, 'Such confident trembling! I can't ape a
King who rules with a flute! They're all flattering
just as if you weren't a professional king.'

'I've Decided,' The King Said, 'That There's Too Much Pomp...

'I've decided,' the King said, 'that there's too much
pomp about being a monarch. This ermine
and this robe and this crown—as if the mere touch
rendered me kingly! I'm going to walk freely
in the streets without ceremony, dressed in
clothes that a subject would wear; simplicity
as my watchword. No airs, no graces, and no
humbug of upper-class pronunciation;
not a word nor a gesture left that could show
monarch in me!'—'So, sire, your abdication
is announced!' shouted Rex. 'Can't you be your age?
All the audience will hiss you off the stage!'

To The Court Came A Thespian…

To the court came a Thespian, of whose fame
everyone spoke. He did a noble hero's
dying speech on the battlefield, would declaim
classical rhetoric till you were cheering
like an ancient republican, or he froze
you with fear at his Caligula choosing
his next victim. 'Superb!' cried the King. 'This man
outshines the best. He's our finest actor!'—
'No, no!' Rex interrupted. 'There's someone can
do much better.'—'There can be no one better:
he excels in his playing! You must be drunk.
Why, 'tis done to the life!'—'Just as you are, nunc.'

*   *   *

'It's That Stunpoll, The King's Jester...

'It's that stunpoll, the King's Jester. Let him lie.'—
'Secrecy first!'—'Nah!—couldn't betray a flea!
Aren't we gentlemen-peasants, ready to die
nobly for all? to end forever the rope
and the axe? to raise up the flag of the free?
Down with the dungeon and the stocks! Long live hope
of a land without law. Burn the block! Knock down
palace and mansion. Snatch off their wigs! Ransack
the cellars and share in the cup!'—'Hear me, clown!'
broke in a voice. 'You've forgotten one drawback:
what of those who might swig too much of the cup?'
'Oh that's nothing, you Fool—we'll just string them up!'

All The Peasants Were Going To The Desert ...

All the peasants were going to the desert.
'Whatever for?' asked Rex; 'there's only sand-dunes
there and cactus and scorpions.'—'Be a convert,
Rex!' they all cried. 'The great Prophet awaits you!—
for there by a palm tree the Prophet communes
all alone!' 'Twas true, save that a faithful few
(now increased) were there too. 'Love the wildest beast!'
cried the unshaven saint. 'Love the savage
with his untainted heart! Love mildest least!
Love the cruellest most! Make your pilgrimage
to the freest of wills! Love the fiercest thing!'—
'Oh, in that case,' said Rex, 'I'll be off to the King.'

On The Scaffold The Outlaw Cried...

On the scaffold the outlaw cried, 'Cowards all!
Law is your whip! So scared you have to obey!
You've got livers of pigeons. I couldn't call
one of you men. Yellow as chicks, all afraid
of a rope, not a will amongst you I'd say.
Glad to see me put away in case I made
myself king of you all! See a man meet death
better than any, who has handled his sword
like a hero, who can shout with his last breath
"Down with all kings!" I'd have killed yours like that lord
that got speared on my spit!'—Up spoke our clown
as the trap fell away: 'That's one king gone down.'

One Tradition The King Had To Keep...

One tradition the King had to keep each year
strictly by custom had long ago lost all
of its meaning. Though everyone there would cheer
just as the King, all naked, entered the sea,
not a soul could say why, or even recall
reasons why that day of all others must be
set apart for a swim without clothes. The feasts
afterwards pleased noble and peasant: roast swan
was enough of a why. This time, as the priests
mumbled nonsense, a child cried, 'He's nothing on!'
But that instant the Fool took up his defence:
'Sssh! You mustn't disturb our Prince's pretence!'

'All These Laws Are A Fraud! ...

'All these laws are a fraud! See what influence
gets you. The pound in a wig beats the penny
every time. You can have all the evidence,
alibis, witnesses you want, but the judge
looks through gold-coloured spectacles. Why, any
law you could name is rigged so no one can budge
who has nothing to prove he's one of the few!
They made the laws just to put fetters on me.
All these laws are shambolic. Nothing is true!'—
'All you've to do is pay the Jester a fee,
and I'll turn every law upside-down,' said Rex;
'I'll be sure to look through my lead-coloured specs.'

'Wha' Oi Carn Stand Is Witual...

'Wha' Oi carn stand is witual! Nuffin but
moanin' an' gwoanin' the same fing over and
over!' said one young cit dressed in his well-cut
buckram. Another in his well-cut buckram
said, 'Wha' Oi carn put up wiv is all these grand
uniforms, sashes an' stars. Finks it makes 'em
do yer nut when yer see 'em!' Said another,
rubbing his horse-brass badge (all of them had one),
'But wha' Oi carn aboide is all their pa'er[1].
Carn speak wivart pu'in'[2] on some overdone
lah-di-da 'ark-at-me!'—Broke in Rex: 'Oi vow,
Arsebishop an' General an' Juke, Oi must bow!'

[1] glottal-stopped *patter*
[2] glottal-stopped *putting*

'He's No More Than The King Of Diamonds, Hearts, Clubs!...

'He's no more than the Kings of Diamonds, Hearts,
Clubs! We're the Spades and we're trumps!' said the peasant
as he picked up the cards. 'I don't give two farts
fizzed by a flea for all the diamonds on
his Crown Jewels, except as repayment
owed to the miners who dug them. If a swan
of an aristocratic bird says she has
given her heart to him, he can't tell if she's
down to earth or she's flighty, the fool! And as
for all his clubs! With them he's a Hercules,
but without, he's a sheep!'—Said Rex: 'Not too quick!
You've forgotten the Joker. He takes the trick!'

'But Vith Marx At The Skvare...

'But vith Marx at the Skvare against Saturn ten
years vill bring all kings to zare doom. Here, you see,
in ze House of ze Bull, wepeated again,
zign of catastrovee: vare kindly planet
wunz in contwawy sense at its apogee,
such contwadiction, to zose who can scan it,
wenders pwoof beyond doubt zat Armageddon
dwaws near, and despots, tywants, kings and nobles
are to tamble in blad, and skies vill wedden,
blazing zare wooin. Zat day of miwacles
vill turn peasant to king!'—'Can't be true!' Rex said.
'You've got one king left over! They're not all dead.'

*   *   *

'Oh, In My Realm, Dear Zar ...

'Oh, in my realm, dear Zar, I don't need to pry.
Take my estates, for example. My steward
knows precisely my wants. My farmers outvie
any of yours, for they don't need to rely
on his guidance. My sheep don't need a shepherd!
Don't find me having always to play the spy
on my own soldiers. I know my general
doesn't require my assistance, nor do his
staff. An army that fights by a natural
genius needs no king when hostilities
start!'—At which there popped up Rex: 'God's wounds!' he swore.
'Why, whatever do we need a monarch for?'

The Commander Of Armies Was Addressing Cadets...

The Commander of Armies was addressing cadets:
'Soldiers today put loyalty first. The King's
orders no one should see as backed up by threats,
courts-martial, punishments, for the King knows each
man's most intimate self. The slightest stirrings,
deep in your being, of your free will to reach
for your happiness, that is what the King knows,
guiding in wisdom to what you truly desire!
Let the King order all that you do. Impose
his will whatever your act!'—'Then you can hire
me to help!' Rex cried. 'The King's orders I'll shout:
Breathe in! Now breathe out! Now breathe in! Now breathe out!'

'Come, A Tale,' Said The King . . .

'Come, a tale,' said the King.—'Once upon a time,'
Rex began, 'nowhere near here, there was a king
who declared to his subjects it was a crime
if they were more or less in height than six foot
(that was *his* height), so anyone measuring
differently had to be chopped short or put
on the rack. How those cheered who escaped with no
more than a graze or a jolt! Then he declared
that all those who weren't bald (he was) had to go,
helped on their way by the axe. Then he compared
noses, eyes, faces—wondering who'd survive,
until he was the only one left alive.'

'Can You Dare To Play Me?' ...

'Can you dare to play me?' said the King.—'How well?'
Rex asked.—'Don't dare to play me badly!'—'If I
did my best (and at acting, note, I excel),
wouldn't your subjects all mistake me for you?'—
'What an insult! They all would identify
Rex, the mad jester! Easy to tell the true
from the false!'—'Dear old nunc, the furless monkey,
strutting in ermine, that's the joke of tonight!
You need genius to act me. You're a flunkey,
nunc, in comparison. To copy you quite
properly, you've set me a teaser, you see:
I must act you acting a king acting me!'

'Does A King Make Up Subjects? ...

'Does a king make up subjects, or do subjects
make up a king?' mused Rex.—'Whatever d'you mean?'
cried the King. 'I'm as real in all respects,
Fool, as the least of them!'—'But there's not a one
who can know you as you, not even your queen:
so everyone must pretend, almost in fun,
that the king that they see is the genuine
one!' said Rex.—'Anyway, I don't make up my
loyal subjects. They're real enough!'—'You'd spin
any old yarn! You don't know then either. Why,
you pretend what you see! What's real is in doubt:
you need me to remind you how to find out.'

At A Tree Planting Ceremony...

At a tree-planting ceremony, every
alderman, dignitary, least official,
had now gathered round, with the committee,
ready to clap as the King wielded the spade
(shining silver and oak, befitting regal
hands). Sad to say, his first load slipped from the blade,
at which Rex burst out laughing, the only one.
All had kept silent, their eyes fixed on the King.
For that moment, he too stood fixed: then—'What fun,
eh? Ha, ha!' Everyone set themselves laughing
at once, but Rex cried, 'Quiet! Thank goodness that tree,
sire, can manage to grow without help from thee!'

'All These Subjects Of Mine...

'All these subjects of mine know me well. I hide
nothing away of my true nature. All's plain
both to me and to them. It's my only pride,
keeping myself as myself, with nought concealed.'—
'Oh but, sire!' interrupted Rex; 'I would feign
lie, but I cannot, for it must be revealed
that a barber here, seeing you for the first
time, was so struck with the poor cut of your beard
he could talk of nought else. Though you were to burst,
sire, with sincerity, it is as I feared,
won't the serf see soft hands, the doctor your skin,
the courtier your faux-pas, and the Fool your grin?'

'What's The Time?' Asked The King...

'What's the time?' asked the King.—'A funny question
that from the ruler!' came the comment from Rex.
'Don't you know?'—'Do you think I'm a magician,
Fool, that can see through a door, or a doctor
of philosophy measuring the reflex
made by a star? or like a sunflower
twist round on my throne, or fashion my nose
into a sundial? Now what's the time?'—'But, sire,
there's no problem for you. Why do you suppose
someone can tell you? No need to make that spire
of a nose do the job. You can make an hour
last a minute and start now. You have the power.'

'Can't Expect Every Tom, Dick And Harry ...

'Can't expect every Tom, Dick and Harry to
walk in at once and demand an audience!
I'd be swamped. So they have to approach me through
proper and formal channels. Anyway, I
understand very little, not a sentence,
uttered by some of these yokels! Let them try
first by asking a clerk to translate their plea
into plain English to their master; then he's
able to put it to his; by each degree
meaning grows into what I can grasp with ease.'—
'Like the paynim,' said Rex, 'who rush to embrace
a new wife without ever seeing her face.'

'Musn't Sit On Your Crown, Sire ...

'Mustn't sit on your crown, sire!'—'You put it there,
Fool!'—'Mind the pricks! Wouldn't want you to become
like the King who got his stuck on his bare
bum. What a rum thing that was! His Fool had spread
glue all over the ermine rim: when his bum
lowered itself onto the close-stool, instead
of the pot, it met crown. And strange to relate,
none of his courtiers noticed. He was upset!
When he shouted and roared, they would imitate
statues, pretend to be deaf, but when he let
off a fart, they all ran as if to obey.
It went on till his Jester gave him away.'

*   *   *

'There's This Fuckin' Wench, See ...

'There's this fuckin' wench, see, and this fuckin' knight,
and he was fuckin' ridin' out one mornin'
for a fuckin' wild boar hunt when a fuckin' sight
took him by fuckin' surprise and nearly knocked 'im
off 'is fuckin' 'orse. There between the fuckin'
trunks he caught sight of a lovely fuckin' limb,
fuckin' whiter than fuckin' snow and as soft,
fuckin' revealin' a fuckin' well-shaped thigh.
As the fuckin' knight watched, the maid fuckin' doffed
last of her fuckin' clothes to bathe in a nearby
fuckin' pool, but the knight—' '—then jumped off his horse,'
went on Rex, 'and had sexual intercourse.'

'My Collection Of Horse-Shoe Nails...

'My collection of horse-shoe nails, although I
say it myself, is the best in the country.
Look at these here for hind hooves: now I defy
anyone anywhere, no matter how rich,
to have matched all this set. See, I have rusty
two-inchers, non-rusty two-inchers—and which
would you pick out of this set for the rarest?
Only an expert like me can really tell
that this notch shouldn't be just here. It's fairest,
all things considered, to admit I excel.
Beat the King anyday!'—'Now I call that cheek,'
complained Rex, 'for this turd of my ass is unique!'

'Oh, You Looked At Me!...

'Oh, you looked at me!' Rex shouted at the King.
'I know you well! You suspect me, innocent
as I am, of high treason! You'll have me swing
soon as a wink!'—'I wasn't looking at you,'
said the King.—Rex snapped back: 'That's no different!
Worse if you weren't looking at me! It's my due!
If you're king you should notice where a subject
is, what he wants, what he needs! He can't find out
on his own. It's a king who has to protect
him 'cause he's ignorant—he's helpless with doubt!
Oh boo hoo! A poor subject is quite forsook
by a king who can't manage to look and not look!'

39

'Have You Heard Of These Poets? ...

'Have you heard of these poets? Finicking fops
skipping in rhymes, flouncing their word-petticoats,
tripping out pretty ditties, dipping milksops
into their dreams! What girlish droops they are, what
perfect slops! Like a baby a poet dotes
dribbling on rattles, on ribbons, and his cot
is his world, full of dumb dolls—let him kiss their
inky lips, clip their letter necks! He can't bend
those straight lines round his back, he can't tickle hair
made out of fancy and paper! He should spend
his time working, not shirking.'—'Could have done worse,'
Rex, the critic, opined: 'It's passable verse.'

'We're The Mohocks—We Rule!...

'We're the Mohocks—We rule! Nobody calls us
names and gets off scot free!' said one of the mob
at the corner. 'If anyone makes a fuss,
sayin' we ain't the great Greats, he'll get a kick
turn 'im inside out. Don't imagine you'll fob
me off, yer fuckin' coward! We're not that thick
we can't prove with our blades we're Kings of the Town.
If you're a Sioux, you'll get scalped soon as you speak!
Up the Mohocks for ever! Everyone down
damned into hell who dares to say we are weak!'
Rex cried out: 'With such fear I am be-shitten!
You deserve every buffalo in Britain!'

'Put A Stick On A Pedestal . . .

'Put a stick on a pedestal—his eyes go
up. Shine a light on the stick—they open wide.
Put a pumpkin on top and a potato
nose of patrician proportions, and his gob
gapes in wonder. A uniform then to hide
what you have nailed as a crosspiece—and he'll bob
like a jack-in-a-box. Fix on some epaulettes
made of the yellowest straw; tie on some tin
to the brim of a crownless hat; add rosettes
snipped out of doilies; loop some string with a pin—
last, a blade made of lath: and you've won his will—
for your enemy's his, that he's mad to kill.'

'The King's Officer's Only Gettin' At Me 'Cause I'm A Hodgkin!' ...

'The King's officer's only gettin' at me
'cause I'm a Hodgkin!'—'Never 'eard the name,' said
the old beadle.—'Oh yes you 'ave! I know thee!'
shouted the dame. 'The King's after another!'
Spoke up Rex: 'Tell me, ma'am, did the King behead
father and mother and sister and brother,
hang your grandad, shoot grandma, lock up your son,
drag off your only daughter to the House of
Convertites where he's forced her to be a nun,
put all your aunts down, sent your uncles above,
locked up neighbours and friends without any bail
till he's shut the whole country up in a gaol?'

'Never Pester Your Pupil With Rules! ...

'Never pester your pupil with rules! Let them
play with the world away from the corruption
of man. Multiplication table, theorem,
grammar, irregular verb, all are so much
an imprisoning ritual, a restriction
fettered on limbs and fingers that ought to touch
anything they can reach to explore. Only
thus can the boy grow to responsible man,
only thus can his innocence in lonely
purity find true growth, flower to a plan
he alone has devised!'—'Look out! Off that sill
he's now pushing a pot to prove his free will!'

'All The Animals Met In An Assembly...

'All the animals met in an assembly,
telling their King, the Lion, that they were not
happy, putting it mildly, with his bounty:
he didn't care a scrap as far as their food
was concerned. So the Lion anxiously got
all his relations together and issued
the command that they all must work on the land,
dawn until sunset, to feed his great people.
But with all the cat tribe now lending a hand
farming, the enemy Man was now able
to go hunting at will. The animals cried
that their King didn't care a scrap if they died.'

*   *   *

Once The Acrobats Came To Court ...

Once the acrobats came to court and cartwheeled,
tumbled and tightrope-walked to the King's applause.
As the last of their tricks the burliest kneeled,
lifted the lighter onto their backs, who then
took the lightest of all. Nodding like seesaws,
up stood the strongest: a pyramid of men.
As he clapped, the King shouted, 'You can't equal
that, Rex!'—'Oh no, but you can. Aren't the strongest
and the best at the bottom and the noodle
wobbling on top the highest and least?'—'Can't twist
all of my words. Go climb up there! Speedily!'—
''Scuse me! I always follow your majesty!'

'Watch Out, Fool, Or I'll Have You Executed!' ...

'Watch out, Fool, or I'll have you executed!'
shouted the King.—'You'll be sorry when they read
out my will, you will!' Rex sobbed. 'I've deputed
you my executor, executioner!
To your lazy young queen goes my lumpy bed:
then she'll get up before noon. Your almoner
gets my ears so he'll hear just how much you told
him to hand over to the poor. Your steward
gets my bobble-and-stick: when he hits an old
man with it hard, it won't bloody his mazzard.
And my pence to your pounds, so they both can go
to pay back to your subjects all that you owe.'

'One Day, Sire, There'll Be Someone Writing About Us...

'One day, sire, there'll be someone writing about
us (and, dear reader, there'll be you reading it!)'—
'No one's listening to you, Rex,' said the King. 'Shout.
Go on. Nobody can hear a word of that!'
'But they'll *read* it, I said (yes, this very bit),
so, as they do, they will know what you're at
is the purest pretence.'—'Don't start that again,
Rex!'—'As they do, they will know which is the real,
an old jester called Rex, who's careful to feign
all that he does, even himself, or ideal
monarchs, putting on airs, as rigid as death.
We are words, which must disappear into breath.'

'So You Think You Can Rule Better Than I Can!' ...

'So you think you can rule better than I can!'
Grinning with certainty of success, the King,
having called all his courtiers, proclaimed his plan,
carefully made, to ennoble Rex the Fool
(and to get his own back by putting a sting
into the gift). 'My lords, our Rex needs to rule
since his wisdom's so great he's corrected me
dozens of times. He must now be invested
with a crown that will suit him! So let him be
King of the Apes, Asses and Wolves! He's jested
far too long!'—Answered Rex: 'Your alms overwhelm!
I've no fancy for ruling *all* of your realm.'

'I Am Tired Of Your Rhymes And Your Word-Twisting! ...

'I am tired of your rhymes and your word-twisting!
Say what you mean. Let us have words that are clear!'
said the King. Rex said, 'Come then, are they misting
over with breath? Give me your ermine to clean
away ignorance. *Clear*, now—let's put a sheer
polish on that for a start! It's got the sheen
of a looking-glass. Windows are for seeing
through, but this *clear*—sorry, your ermine's got caught
on that sharp *cl-*!'—'Let go, you Fool!'—'I'm freeing
you, don't you see? It'll come loose as a thought
in a trice. To use *one* sense is quite absurd:
you are dumb if you say we can't twist a word.'

'Have You Heard Of The Man, Nunc...

'Have you heard of the man, nunc, who, while at the play,
thought that the wicked king really was trying
to deflower the maiden and rightaway
leapt on the stage and ran the poor Thespian
through before they could stop him, terrifying
all the spectators? Take that poor ruffian
as that would-be assassin of you last spring.
Then, have you heard of the Roman emperor
who thought plays needed more than mere pretending:
when it was time for the sturdy warrior
to be stabbed, a poor knave's blood had to be spilt.
Take that emperor, nunc, as fooled to the hilt.'

Then The General Cleared Away The Dinner Plates...

Then the General cleared away the dinner
plates. 'Here was I.' He put down the pepper-pot
on the tablecloth; then with the salt-cellar—
'Here was the foe. The mustard, sire, is the Horse.
When the enemy tried hard with musket shot
here to reduce our pressure, I brought a force
of your gallant Hussars suddenly across
just by the vinegar, and so massacred
every man! We won with the minimal loss!'—
'In the assault,' chanted Rex, 'how you've mustered
all you meet! how you've peppered all the gory!
What a spice you have sprinkled on your glory!'

As He Rose From The Throne

As he rose from the Throne, Rex with fastidious
care wiped his arse on the velvet canopy;
then he bent to the cushion with a curious
stare, held his nose, winced away grimacing
in a naive amazement like a monkey.
'Oh, to be king!' he cried. 'No embarrassing
painful havings-to-wait! no frustration of
farts! I can foist what I like on my people.
I'm not one who can stand constipation of
impulse. Get shot of the lot with least trouble
and let others put up with what's odious.
That's the reason the Throne is commodious.'

Rex Asked, 'Why is a Raven Like A Writing-Desk?' ...

Rex asked, 'Why is a raven like a writing-
desk?'—'I don't know,' said the King. 'Is it because
there are quills on both? How's that for a fighting
answer?'—'No good. Try again.'—'Because it's there
that an author in order to win applause
must use his talons?—'Worse and worse.'—'It's unfair!
I can pun just as well as you! What about
this one then? Don't you see open bills on both?'—
'That they're *different* how can you have any doubt?'—
'Well, what's the answer then, Fool? I'll take my oath
I'm as good as you.'—'If we call things the same
'cause the King says they are, then you'll be to blame.'

*   *   *

'Can't Speak Proper, These Aristocrats!...

'Can't speak proper, these aristocrats! They're too
daft to be able to follow a simple
rule what anyone can. Even a child can do
better than them. Everybody knows you say
were in "I were just thinkin' like"; no trouble
either to say *was* in "They was late today".
They're right daft an' all.'—'Peasants are trapped by their
lack of ability to articulate
the King's English. They cannot speak with due care:
rules count for nothing. They cannot conjugate
an auxiliary properly. I despair
of them saying "I *was* thinking", or, "They *were*".'

'The King's Herdsman One Day Lost One Of The Fine Cows...

'The King's herdsman one day lost one of the fine cows—it was stolen or fell down a well or disappeared in the woods. The number of kine (hundred-and-one) was well known to the monarch, whose inspection was due. The swain in terror rushed for his pig. First, he branded the King's mark on its haunches, and stuck two candle-snuffer horns by its ears, and slung his three-legged pot underneath its back legs, then dragged this duffer heifer among the cattle. "But this is not a cow!" cried the King.—'No, sire, you're mistaken. This cow is renowned for excellent bacon.'

'Once The King of The Asses Had As A Burden Baskets Of Salt ...

'Once the King of the Asses had as a burden
baskets of salt. They were extremely heavy—
ignorant Man was too stupid to reckon
how much a donkey could carry, but the King
was far wiser. A fine opportunity
offered itself. At a ford he went swimming
till the salt had dissolved. So He passed a law
ordering every ass to plunge in and swim
at a ford. All His subjects were filled with awe
hearing such wisdom: they all hee-hawed a hymn
to His Law. But they wondered why He'd been crowned
when all those who'd had burdens of wool were drowned.'

'Have You Heard The Tale
Of King Oh And King Egg?' ...

'Have you heard of the Tale of King Oh and King
Egg?' once asked Rex of His Majesty.—'I can't
recall hearing it, Rex.'—'As twins, resembling
each other perfectly, no one was able
to tell which was which. Now Oh always wished to grant
freely their subjects' requests—you could wheedle
what you liked out of him—for they shared the throne,
he and his brother. Now Egg got so cross at
all this softness of Oh's—boiled hard as a stone,
he was—that in the end, Oh came to say that
no more pleas could be heard, and Egg was to blame:
but a rebel stabbed Oh to death just the same.'

Rex Sat Down At The Tavern Table...

Rex sat down at the tavern table and took
out a large stone from his pouch, placing it
before him. He pretended to start to cook,
rolling it round, not-kneading it, not-chopping
it, not-smelling it, brows raised, not-sprinkling it
over with salt and pepper, and then dropping
it, secretly wiping it on his motley,
frowning at laughs, not-stirring it as it fried
on the not-hot not-gridiron; then he really
jumped and began to shake his finger and tried
to cool no-burn, but knocked down stone and no-fat.
Out went stone as he screamed, 'I couldn't eat that!'

'I've No Time For Those People...

'I've no time for those people who make out that
rank and tradition mean nothing.'—'Said the Ice
to the Fire,' said Rex. The Marquis glared at
him, but went on. 'He is a Machiavel
who as ignorant upstart won't see the price
breaking of custom entails.'—'Said the Eggshell
to the Spoon at the King's breakfast.'—'He must be
brought to see title as conferring a right
of itself: every rebel who shouts "I'm free!
Down with restraint!" is damning himself in spite!'—
'As their paths crossed, both heading straight for the brine,
thus said the Lemmings to the Gadarene Swine.'

'Shall I Tell You The Tale Of The Two Weathercocks?' ...

'Shall I tell you the Tale of the Two Weathercocks?'—
'Yes, since I can't stop you.'—'A Rook alighted
next to one, and the Cock said to him, "Your flocks,
driven by chance here and there, cannot match my
prompt obedience. My lords, the Winds, have varied
many a time, but I've never missed their eye!"
The insulted Rook flew to another spire:
there was a Cock with a big head and arrows
on his tail. "Giddy Rook, why aren't you afire,
deep in your heart, with rebellion, when our foes
are the Winds? Look at me! Oppose the System
all the time!" But the Rook flew off to freedom.'

'There's A Beautiful Bottle That Nobody Ever Can Fill Or Ever Empty...

'There's a beautiful bottle that nobody
ever can fill or ever empty. A quill
never writes though they dip it continually
into the blackest of ink. There's a blanket
never warms anybody, and sheets so chill
no one can sleep between them. There are velvet
cushions no one will pillow his head upon,
goblets of fine gold that never hold wine,
candlesticks without flames, no bristles on
some magic broom sticks, handles without a sign
of a drawer, some bolts that always bang free,
and some locks tightly shut for which there's no key.'

'Don't Believe I Exist,' ...

'Don't believe I exist,' said Rex, 'nor do you.'—
'Nonsense!' the King replied. 'There you are as plain
as the print on a page.'—'What? just a long queue
cramped in with gawky limbs, blank circle faces,
hunched-up aitches, d's and b's bulging with strain
w's concertina'd into spaces
much too small for them, x's always crossed out,
c's with a hole they can never mend—and you say
that these *mean*? Why, this face is printed with doubt,
now, at the moment it moves, and this hand may
go so cleverly wriggling over a sheet
about me, but the writing's never complete.'

*   *   *